This Dust

MAXINE LINNELL

SOUNDSWRITE
PRESS

First published in 2017 by
SOUNDSWRITE PRESS
52 Holmfield Road
Leicester LE2 1SA

www.soundswritepress.co.uk

ISBN: 978-0-9550786-9-9

Copyright © Maxine Linnell, 2017

Cover image: *Benn* by Ellen Stewart

Typeset in Gills Sans MT & Cambria
Front cover font IM Fell French Canon.
Fell Types are digitally reproduced by
Igino Marino www.iginomarino.com

Printed and bound by Lightning Source UK Ltd

Thanks are due to the editors of the following magazines and anthologies where some of the poems or earlier versions first appeared: *Acumen, Envoi, Fin, Futures anthology* (Pewter Rose Press, 2011), *Soundswrite anthology* (Soundswrite Press, 2011 and 2013), *The Book of Love & Loss* (The Belgrave Press, 2014), *Welcome to Leicester* (Dahlia Publishing, 2016).

CONTENTS

I

Night sky	7
51595	8
Lido	9
Meat	10
Dance out of time	11
If you lay next to me now	12
Pixellated	14
Cloak	16
White freesias	17
Threads	18
Fish strawberry wasp	19
Coat hooks	20
Looking for Teresa	21

II

Introduction	24
And now he is	25
The trowel he made in metalwork	26
Flying	27
Knots	28
Chocolate	29
He fell out of time	30
Only you	31
Brick Lane	32
Hair	33
He	34
Waking	35
Without-you	36
Soundings	38
Question	40
Vanitas	41
Omega	42
Five years on	43

III

For Elliot	47
Beeman	48
Beach lessons	49
Names	50
Growing	51
Fishing for eternity	52
Presents	53
Move	54
Stuff	55
Acknowledgements	57

I

Night sky

That Hartland summer night
when we looked up and they were so close
and bright we picked them off the sky,
star by sizzling star.

They smelled so milky-sweet
that we popped them in our mouths
and they fizzed and fizzed
and made our eyes glow,
our fingers tingle
and our toes twitch and dance.
Made us write poems,
rewrite our lives.

51595

The Co-op on Uppingham Road was two quick stops on the bus
or a good ten-minute walk on my short legs. She wrote me a list,
not long, but I worried in case I got it wrong. I took her old bag
and the man in brown overalls wrapped things up in brown paper
with a rip of sellotape – jagged at the ends. He picked the stub
of yellow pencil from behind his ear, listed the prices, ruled a line
at the end then added up, carrying over the shillings and pence.
I worried that I wouldn't have enough and would have to choose
to leave the bread, the ham or the eggs, but I wouldn't let go of the jam.

He asked me my number and I still know it, even though
my phone number's gone. There was no printed receipt
spelling out the change, but a small coloured ticket
torn with perforations for the divi. If there were pennies left,
I'd go to the fishmonger's next door for a twist of prawns,
lug the bag to Humberstone Park, sit on a swing, pull off
the heads and tails, smell the salt and taste the far-off sea.

Lido

Lined up on the lido beach
like stranded fish, we sunsoak
through chlorine haze,
giggle and tell stories,
daring boys to notice.

Drowsy with heat, I barely
stir when a young male voice
says my back is red
with a sticky offer
to spread suncream.

I leave my head
on my forearms.
With cool hands
stroking my skin,
for a moment
I don't care who he is.

Meat

We walk to the pool on Vestry Street in twos,
herded by teachers front and back,
lugging kit bags stuffed with towels and swimsuits
up the bridge, over the hill behind the station.
And there's that abattoir smell.

Beyond wide-open doors
we see cream and red bodies hook-hung,
men in blood-white aprons swing carcasses
so they bump each other
like the cows they were once,
hustled to market, huffing steam into cold air.

The stench spreads out, shadows us.
We hold our breaths and noses
as the men wolf-whistle us on to the pool,
where chlorine stings eyes and throats
and we huddle into changing-rooms,
three girls to one small bay
bumping each other with elbows and knees.

Dance out of time

You made all the perfect moves
so I recalled that special dance,
loved your lean body inside out
wondering if it might be the last
I knew.

You danced me right through
before going back to blue.

Strange. The mirror showed the girl
I'd been, bright skin, green longing eyes
as if she'd waited there till now, still
seventeen behind the lived-through lines
I knew.

I thought you saw her too
before turning back to blue.

We planned, built castles of our lives,
sand drifting through a child's small hand;
the dancers were danced out of time
faster than blur of feet on land
and for a dazzling moment flew

I knew
before dropping back to blue.

If you lay next to me now

If you lay next to me now
I couldn't stretch out my legs and arms,
you'd ask what I'm thinking,
you'd want something, silent or out loud,
you'd want to listen to the radio.

If you lay next to me now
you could be snoring.
You'd take up all the duvet.
I'd only have one side
for the piles of books.

If you lay next to me now
you'd want to watch bad films.
You'd want sex before or after I did –
worse, not at all –
you'd be bored, angry, ill.

If you lay next to me now
you'd be afraid.
You'd be afraid of dying
and I'd be frightened too
of losing you.

If you lay next to me now
you'd be almost an old man,
because I'm almost an old woman.
Your eyes might blur.
You'd remember me like new.

If you lay next to me now
you'd have a warm hand
on my hip or my shoulder,
or your leg would touch mine.
You'd know to stay quiet for a while

if you lay next to me now,
then you'd curl up close to my back,
breathe on my neck.
I'd put the pencil down,
turn round. We'd smile.

Pixellated

I didn't mean it. That bit when you said,
or wrote – *you were always the one
for Paul* – and I said – *you were always
the one for me* – and even though
we were chatting on facebook I heard
the message drop into your mind
and leave a mark. Shouldn't have,
it's just so easy, sitting here.
Paul died last week
and I thought I'd broken
some etiquette about dead ex-lovers
where I should have said *yes,
he was always the one for me*,
even though he wasn't, and I
should have been gathered
in a spotlight of lost loves
and longings and I should have
gazed down, tears pixellating
my eyes, even though we were on
messenger and you wouldn't see.
And of course I was sad Paul had
died, of course, we were close
for a while, and he came into
my thoughts. But I wasn't sad
how I'd be if we were really
the one for each other –
I hadn't seen him for twenty years,
but then I haven't seen you for forty
and what you and I had didn't last
long. You were quiet for a while,

then you came back and I
remembered your impressions
of Neil Young, who I didn't even like,
how we laughed with the others,
John, Pete, and Bob sometimes,
read out our poems in a Birmingham
bedsit, staked our claims to each other.
But I did. Mean it. I think I might have.
And now you know.

Cloak

There's a don't-see-me cloak hanging in my wardrobe
sequinned with middle-aged woman designs.
It keeps me warm and dry, but it's starting to stick
even when it's hot, and I'm afraid
one day it won't come off at all.

White freesias

Dad was a quiet man, worked in the bank,
came home by bus for lunch, liked peace and rest,
loved Shakespeare, words, his paper, little more.
He drowned inside himself. His lungs filled up.
It took them years, far longer than he wished
and doctors promised. Wheelchair and coffin
were almost booked. But he went on, slower
and deafer, finishing crosswords, filling hours
with small tasks in the house, while all the time
the waters rose, flooding out his breath.

Later, it helped me breathe to see him dead.
No fight, the dark lines on his face smoothed out.
Alive – he could not be near scented flowers.
Dead – white freesias for him, ease at last.

Threads

A summer spent hunting the best price
for panama hat, beret, shirts, tie,
skirt hung on the knee, navy knickers,
long white socks, sensible shoes.

The nametapes live at the bottom
of the sewing box. Armed with glasses
and thimble, you sewed them
on netball shirt and hockey shorts.
They smelled of not knowing the rules.
They were too white to hide behind.

Today I sit with you, sewing your name
on underwear thin with washing.
You say this new home
is like the boarding school you longed for,
but not quite.

The needle pierces skin.
I cut the thread
with my teeth.

Fish strawberry wasp
for Joy

Up to her knickers in stream,
she caught tadpoles
through bent light,
carried them home
by a string handle
to free in the garden pond.

Strawberries,
hulled, sugared,
boiled, packed in
with gingham covers,
to spread
on home-baked scones.

Her hand shook.
A wasp
trapped against the window
might find a way
to sting
through glass.

This summer she is lost for words.
The simple ones –
fish
strawberry
wasp –
slip far down

too deep for catching.

Coat hooks

Roomy kagoule, sized for shape-shifts,
blue for sky-blending on those day-long hikes
with picnics at our backs.

Unremarkable red fleece
flew to Africa and back –
saw glittering nights from six to six.

Velvet jacket, short and tight,
tried on in the mirror's eyes
and then replaced, unused.

Long winter wool from a mother's
icy funeral. Wind sliced that coat through –
left tattered rags inside.

Definite black, all belt, zip,
buttons and asymmetry,
ready for action, braced for anything.

Disappearing soft green-blue
weightless as tissue paper –
snuggles at black's sleeve.

Behind them that brown suede waistcoat,
danced stiff, sweat-dark, long fringes gone,
back scrawled with sequins – Good Times.

Looking for Teresa

I've looked for you everywhere in Avila, seen pictures
in the catacombs, walked where you walked, understood
your images of walls and inner castles in this town
with huge stone walls and red mountains beyond.

But you've eluded me – I've found history and decoration,
a tourist draw, the little train that drags them round the sites
so they don't need to walk, the beggars holding out their hands
by church gates, the streets and squares named after you.

You waited twenty years for Him – I've been here two days
before I find this place, a small side chapel cluttered with gold.
A figure of you in your nun's robes leans out from the nave.
There's a narrow bench where I watch the tourists come and
                                                               look and go.

But none of this draws me. It's the floor, grey stone, only a few
                                                              feet square,
where something happens, something to keep me here for
                                                              several hours,
something I can't explain, which changes me. Under this chapel
is the room where you were born.

I find you here,
in this stillness,
this dust.

II

for Benn Linnell 1973–2010

Introduction

My son Benn was born on 25th August 1973. It was a difficult birth. In his teens he developed epilepsy. He became an artist, mentor, curator, builder and project manager. Benn was living with his partner Gayna in their flat on Brick Lane in London when he died on 17th November 2010. A seizure caused his death.

And now he is

The birthing tongs,
doing what being might have done
in its own time,
have marked their metallic shape
on his still-sliding skull plates.
He's bruised from out to in,
and when he finds our world
he lets us know
how hard his way has been.
He seems too tender to touch,
even to whisper a welcome.
He might break at a smile.
The midwife picks him up like porcelain.
Her hand fits round his hurting head.
He's beautiful, she says,
and now he is.

The trowel he made in metalwork

The smooth wooden handle fits in my palm,
the blade curve deep, painted blue at the tip.
Rivets pin it to a thin stem drilled into the wood.

Like most things he made, this trowel lasted.
A while ago the steel ring slipped
off the handle. It dangles round the stem
and won't be forced back on.

It's like a manacle. Or maybe a charm.

Flying

The video came in the post,
with an Australian postmark.
There was no note.
Clunked into the player, it ran. I watched him
climb into the plane, sit waiting to go.
He looked at the camera,
grinned behind the goggles.
Don't worry, Mum!
He dropped, held by a bigger man,
flew, landed, rolled on his back
spread-eagled with delight,
laughing, laughing.

Knots

Sometimes I'd sit on a sofa
and he'd find me, lower
his leanness and his height
onto the floor. I'd pull
gently at the black curls on
his head, springing them back into place
and he'd ask me to loosen
his shoulders. I'd find the knots,
he'd want pressure so hard my
thumbs ached, so I'd use knuckles,
fingers, and he'd sigh out loud, click his neck
and laugh. I'd have to stop for the pain
reaching from him to my fingers and thumbs,
rest my hands on his hair, lean forward,
hold him safe. Then he'd be standing up again,
ready for whatever came next,
smiling a shrugging dance.

Chocolate

I got to St Pancras, cold and dark.
We hugged. He asked me what I'd like.
A really good hot chocolate.
He took my arm, we walked to the taxi rank,
talked and laughed in the back until we
spilled out onto the pavement by
a Salon de Thé with lacy curtains,
yellow light splashing the windows,
steam on the glass.

The finest hot chocolate
served in porcelain cups.
The hiss of steam from the kitchen.
His way of charming the waitress.
His knack of finding the very best table.
His smile on delivering perfection.

He fell out of time

while others kept hold,
found himself lying somewhere
back hurting, twisted,
tongue swollen, bitten,
mind in a different place.

Only you

'T'sonly me, sung through the phone,
you – who could never be only you –
who could be only and more than part of me
apart from, away from *'t'sonly you*
and when I said *how are you*
– as you do – and when I said
how are you, only you,
you said I'm getting there –
and I repeated – *getting there* –
almost close enough down the phone
but not quite close enough,
getting there – wherever there is,
sometimes I said – *wherever that is, there,*

and I know you were getting there
– you are – because there is no there
or there was no there, then, before now.
And now you were there – then – you were there
when there was nowhere else to be.

Brick Lane

You moved into Brick Lane,
that industrial room, pipes and wires exposed,
your hopes intact, promises piled
in cardboard boxes lining the walls.

You could cycle round that
vast living room and you did,
crowing with homeliness
and your smiling life.

Six months on, you have gone.
We stack the boxes again.
Now they are loaded with tears.
They sag and teeter.

Dreams litter the floor. We sweep them
away, sweep until it's over.
Hand back the keys.
The evening sun dances on dust.

Hair

First, that big hurt
newborn head.

Long curls, the nursery said
they'd cut them short.

Henna for orange at camp,
cropped way past curls.

Dreadlocks overflowed skin
shaved around the ears.

White specks settled in before thirty,
like slowest snow.

Brushed the wrong way in his coffin,
warmer than his skin.

He

He – it is him – lies there
but lying there sounds like an action
and this is pure absence of activity.

He has been lain there
by others,
dressed by them,
his hair smoothed back,
unlike himself.
Blue pools patch his face.
He is all lack of motion,
all lack.
Even the air around him
is still and cold.

Waking

Waking up to you dead each day
I have to find a way down
the length of day corridor
without more bruises,
without knocking at scabs,
bleeding in too many places,
which is hard when
the floor lurches underfoot,
bucks at every step.

Without-you

You are a-part-of-me.
You are apart
from me and now you're dead.
You are a-dead-part-of-me.
You are apart from me,
and you-having-been
are a part of me-still-being.

The hot, damp pinknesses of you,
waffle-blanketed, all a-go.
The breath of you,
the smell of you,
the life of you squirming in my arms,
the cold dry purpling of you there – gone.
The death of you.

Sitting with without-you
for so many hours,
without-you seeps into me,
settles in,
makes itself at home.

Without-you is how I see.
I taste without-you on my tongue,
in the back of my throat,
like nothing else
but without-you.

There's nothing soft about without-you,
nothing sweet.
Without-you thrashes, clangs.
Without-you is hoarse.
Blood streaks its eyes.
Spit soaks its skin.
Without-you is wild
through and through.

I won't tiptoe round without-you.
I'll roar without-you till my throat sores.
Without-you lifts me,
spins, drops,
and I feel each bone break,
and broken.

Without-you is all a-go.
Without-you squirms in my arms,
howls unblanketed.

Soundings

When he died yesterday, we hardly knew
what today was. When he died last week,
on Wednesday, shock gave way to sobbings
in the night. We wouldn't believe a month
could drag us from him, and him from us.
We were alive, and he had gone – but we woke
up still discovering. He'd gone, through each
long night, and every single dawn. Christmas
that wasn't Christmas came and went.
We got through. Time kindly took the day,
in the end.

Two months and the seventeenth came round again,
but this seventeenth was Monday. The sounding
echoed. This distance wasn't welcome.
He died – yesterday, two months ago. Two months
and a day ago we were all together, we tell each other,
tell anyone who'll bear to listen. We were together.
I hugged him at the station, my face against his coat in the
November dark, wished I could stay to wave, and left.
Left.

Towards each seventeenth, the pain sharpens
its teeth. Relief when it's done, but then no
break each eighteenth when we wake.
There's Mother's day, our birthdays.
We can't believe it's six months, seven,
and at eight begin to dread the twelfth,
his birthday hanging in between, how can we,
cake, candles, balloons dusty, dry and grey.

One year. The would, the should have beens.
How can it be one year. Not a question, an
impossibility. One year, we tell ourselves. Not
listening now. How could we hear that told.
One year.

The second year. The echo takes longer to return.
It's possible to say the thirteenth and the fourteenth
month. Eighteen months and the half-year
breaks through. Then it gets harder to count,
until two. That wretched two. For three months
after two, it's just over two years on.
Refusing to let him go, again.
Another loss.

And now a different way to make the sound. Now,
he died. November 2010. It was a Wednesday. Some
far-off bell, sounding. November, 2010. He died.
That won't change from now. Some far-off
cracked bell. Sounding.
Still sounding.

Question

Hiding among the crates of
cynic and boxes of disbeliever,
gathering cobwebs and dust,
there's a question. It glows
when touched by sunlight,
waits to be noticed. I've
walked past so many times,
looked away, focussed on anything but.

The question's waited long enough,
leaps out, its face bumping
into mine. I can't break free.
So tell me, will I see him again?
Hear his laugh, touch the rough of his hands,
rumple those tight black curls, meet
his searching eyes?

The question unwinds itself, stretches,
yawns, climbs into the light, sits,
looks at me, just as he might,
leans towards me, smiles.

Vanitas
after Luigi Miradori
Wellcome Trust 2013 exhibition, Death: A self-portrait.

A baby's skin shines bright against black, front-lit.
He's naked, asleep, sprawled on his side.
His fair curls tuck behind an ear.
He's dimpled and creased,
his cheeks are full and pink.
His navel dents his stomach. His hips rest
on a red cushion, velvet, braided.
His upper arm tangles in white silk.
His elbow points out.
He almost hugs a darkened adult skull,
eye sockets black.
His head lies on its crown.
His face kisses its forehead.
Without the skull
he would fall, wake, wail.

Omega
The date of death, a capital O, the last in a series, a Swiss watch

Buzz Aldrin wore his to the moon –
    watch out.
James Bond wouldn't be
without that Omega –
    watch how you go.

Photos stand behind glass,
every fixed pixel frozen.
We lost you on my watch.
    Mothers are always on watch.

Your Omega is on my wrist –
    keep watch, keep safe, keepsake.
The balance wheel still flickers,
the mainspring stays unsnapped,
the face uncracked,
the hands unstopped.
This watch warms to my pulse
as it once did to yours.

I'll keep watch,
    your watchdog,
    your last,
    your Omega.

Five years on

I choose you, clambering life,
choose you to kill me in your own sweet time
not mine, choose you to make what you want of me,
choose the workings of you that I can't sort
into story or sense. This story won't tread
through a well-known script marked out
for flaws and cracks and inconsistencies.

This script is unfamiliar – here
life blunders on, ignoring
any clumsy pain it's caused.

This script – so raw that it's a naked page –
I choose you – this page with no lines,
no words, no letters, no marks,
nothing to follow, nowhere for the eye to rest –
no page even – those crisp white edges
hold far too much shape.

The heart is back.
It can't be closed forever.
Life lumbers on,
and there are children to love.

III

For Elliot
born 18th November 2011

The rain's slipped into mizzle,
mist, shades of wet air.
The wind's up, the river's mad, muddy swirls
catch on a stone, a rusting shopping trolley.

We tramp under the bridge,
trying our voices for the boom,
open the gate, flounder through mud,
stamp in puddles. You pick a leaf
off your shining yellow wellies, carefully,
then check your hands for dirt,
rub them together.

We stride the bumpy meadow, hoping for ducks
and woodpeckers, maybe a kingfisher.
Two dripping horses in dirty coats
under leafless trees let you stroke their noses.
We climb the rise like Everest.

Your hand's in mine. You hold my cracked life
light in your small palm. I hug you
right through your wet coat.

Beeman

Shading our eyes, we see the bees.
They drift around a corner of the roof,
hover, drop to flowers for supplies
and glide back up. They could be stinging now.

The beeman brings binoculars.
Bumblebees. The May full moon's
enticed them here to play and mate
among the gutters. *A gift*, he says.
*They've come to show you there's a crack
in a tile or somewhere in the soffits.*

The queen's taking her pick.
Bee testosterone sends them wild.
It won't last long, he says.
*They're gone by June, the nest too.
They'll do no harm up there.*

Standing by him, I see the gift of bees,
appreciate their dance, their crumbling nest.
Wild bumblebees chasing the moon.

Beach lessons

First choose your beach. Be sure you're alone,
best to be there soon after dawn
before the others come to fill
the space you will want smooth and clear.

Then find the shelf the tide leaves last,
where sea has left its jumble sale
of treasures, and pick out one stick,
long as a walking pole, light to carry.

Scramble down the shelf, tracking the stones
as they shrink beneath your feet, until
you reach the level sand. You'll need
the stretch playing tag with the sea. Find it.

Stand in that place. Test out the stick
in your hand, measure length, weight,
strength, if it's bending or brittle.
Look out to sea. Look back to the land.

Then write or draw whatever comes.
Stop. Breathe. When it's time, walk on.
Throw the stick away or keep it.
You may or may not remember.

Names

We carved out these sections of the meadows,
named them gardens, laid down shrubs
and trees, paths, lawns and flowers.
We called them ours, as if the birds
flying over needed an invitation,
as if the rabbits wouldn't eat the lettuce
without permission, as if the fox would know
that running a path down the bank left
too definite a mark. The squirrels know
fences are raised to show their tricks
to advantage. When the sparrowhawk
waits in the magnolia, still for hours,
it's clearly demeaning itself in the domestic.
We think a heron fished my neighbour's pond,
but who can tell. Last week I watched
a rat, with its private entrance to my
compost bin, wander between the bird bath
and sweet peas, as if it wasn't vermin.
They live here; I visit now and then.

Growing

In spite of everything I do to them, they grow.
In spite of being sown at will and at the wrong time, in wobbling rows.
In spite of random watering and more random sun.

In spite of winds, pigeons, ants, and slugs who don't know how to
                                          share, they soldier on.
If they're lucky they might get a sprinkle of food, a splash of
                                          comfrey tea,
the hoe scraped round their roots. They're well neglected.

But here they come, the buds on the runner beans,
broad bean pods erect on their stems,
onion and garlic spikes, courgettes bursting through,

mangetouts poking out from their tendrils. Not to mention the herbs,
chives in full flower, lemon balm, fennel full of aphids and ladybirds,
mint wandering about, sage, thyme, rosemary putting on a spread.

If I believed in God, I might give him a nod for all his bounty.
I don't, but I'll dance the garden, sharing out the praise.

Fishing for eternity

We live here landlocked,
dreaming of Skegness and Bournemouth,
pretending in swimming pools,
leaping off Abbey Park bridge into unknown depths
to save supermarket trolleys from drowning.

Slow River Soar with its unjust name crawls past,
dust clinging to its surface.
We spend minutes watching each mote drag by.
Ducks give us our waves, hot winds fan us
with an ozone ghost, faint memory of salt.

One birthday we go to Belgrave Hall gardens,
eat samosas, onion bhajis and apples,
lick oil and spices from our fingers,
light candles to float downriver
and chant them off to faraway sea.

They founder on débris at the water's edge.
Three boys arrive to ask what we're doing.
Fishing for eternity, you say,
sailing to the end of the earth
where land runs headlong into ocean.

The boys look uneasy,
they ask if it's allowed.
We give them the apples we have left,
and leave them
bombing the candles with stones.

Presents

I gave you a smile –
you pawned it.

I gave you blackbird song –
you took out a patent.

I gave you a button –
you undid it.

Give me an answer,
I'll find a question.

Give me everything,
you won't miss it.

Give me nothing,
I'm content with less.

Move

The house is a stage, set for exits.
The play's over, but the props hang around,
make weight marks in the carpets
for the next players to find.

Home shrivels to boxes in a box,
shadows of belongings,
a past named in felt-pen scribbles on tape,
seamed over so it won't
slip out and bare its teeth.

One room is so stuffed with stuff
I can only open the door
and marvel where it all came from,
wonder where it will go.
There's no way in.

The cupboards are empty
as they've never been.
Windows stare,
lights hang naked,
ashamed of their own bulbs.

Home. It's not the creak
of that landing floorboard;
not the sheets and pillows
and the dismantled double bed;
not that light filtering the curtains,
splashing the walls I painted,
the patch I missed.

Stuff

I never saw the woman who lived opposite.
She left soon after I moved in with my complete boxed past,
scrabbled to make sense of this new place.

I came with far too much. She left with little, for a care home.
I think I might have liked her –
the magnolia, countless terracotta pots

spilling on gravel, paint cracked on the leaning gate,
that green they thought would last
back in the fifties.

Her friends begin to clear the house,
offer a pick of the pots, some plants.
I take three, stifling the urge for more.

They work slowly, take carloads, dump
a tumble dryer in the front. It caught fire
when they tried to turn it on.

She dies. Skips arrive.
Her life heaps in, heads for the tip.
I wonder what matters, when I'll follow.

Acknowledgements

My daughter Kate, son-in-law Liam, and grandsons Elliot and Will are responsible for there being a future after Benn died. Elliot was born a year and a day later. My brother Dave is part of the structure which has made things possible. My closest friends were there through it all, and Benn's partner Gayna is still important in my life. *'So much love'* – the words on the marker at Benn's grave, the sense of his life, and the stuff which survives and was there through the hardest years.

The charity SUDEP Action (Sudden Unexpected Death in Epilepsy) was available from the start to help us try to make sense of what was happening, and The Laura Centre in Leicester gave me a place where anything could be felt, and said, and accepted.

Lightning Source UK Ltd.
Milton Keynes UK
UKOW01f2339130717
305206UK00004B/22/P